Arts & Crafts

BLOCK PRINTING

Susie O'Reilly

With photographs by Zul Mukhida

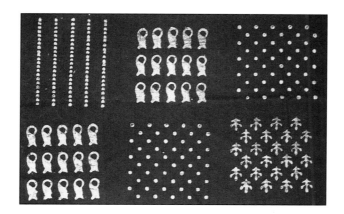

Wayland

Titles in this series

BATIK AND TIE-DYE
BLOCK PRINTING
MODELLING
PAPER MAKING
STENCILLING
WEAVING

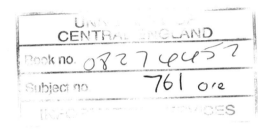
Frontispiece *Detail of a piece of block printed fabric from India.*

© Copyright 1993 Wayland (Publishers) Ltd

First published in 1993 by
Wayland (Publishers) Ltd
61 Western Road, Hove
East Sussex BN3 1JD, England

Editor: Anna Girling
Designer: Jean Wheeler

British Library Cataloguing in Publication Data
O'Reilly, Susie
Block Printing.—(Arts & Crafts Series)
I. Title   II. Series
761

ISBN 0 7502 0682 9

Typeset by Dorchester Typesetting Group Ltd, Dorchester, Dorset, England
Printed and bound by Lego, Italy

CONTENTS

Words printed in **bold** appear in the glossary.

GETTING STARTED

Block printing is an ancient craft. Four thousand years ago, the Egyptians were using carved blocks to print patterns on **fabric**. By the sixth century AD, the craft was widely practised in many countries, including India, China, Japan, Mexico, Peru and Persia.

In the Middle East, the ancient **civilizations** of the Sumerians and the Babylonians used carved surfaces as **seals** for stamping and impressing marks into clay **tablets**. Paper was not invented until the first century AD and it was not widely available in Europe until the fifteenth century. After this time block printing became an important way of reproducing words and illustrations for early books. Artists were involved in drawing the pictures, but skilled craftsmen were responsible for copying the drawings on to blocks, carving and printing.

▲ *This imprint was made using an ancient Babylonian carved seal. The seal is cylinder-shaped (like a soup-tin) so that it could be rolled over soft clay.*

There are many ways of using block printing. You may wish to print the same **image** over and over again, on one sheet, to produce a repeating pattern. Or you can print the same image on different sheets of paper, to make a matching set, called a **run**. You may simply want to make a picture, exploring the special effects that can be produced using printing blocks.

◀ *This is an illustration from a fifteenth-century book. It was printed in Germany using wood blocks. A different block would have been used for each colour.*

▲ Fabrics, like silk and cotton, can be decorated with block printed patterns.

◄ The famous artist Pablo Picasso block printed this big, bold portrait, called Woman with a Hat.

To get started you will need the following equipment.

Craft knife
Cutting board
Scissors

Small wooden blocks or empty matchboxes
Plasticine and rolling pin
Pieces of polystyrene
PVA glue
Nail varnish remover

Printing inks (see page 16)
Powder paints or ready-mixed paints
Wallpaper paste
Washing-up liquid

Overalls and rubber gloves (to protect your skin and clothes)

Metal or glass sheet (such as a baking tray) to use as an inking slab
Deep tin lid or margarine tub and foam sponge to make into a printing pad
Rollers
Paint brushes

Fabric (plain cotton)
Paper and card (a range of types and colours)

Old newspapers (to protect work surfaces)

An old blanket, sheet of polythene and masking tape to make a printing table

Drying rack or line

Needles, thread and a sewing machine

Word processor

Sketchbook and camera

BLOCK PRINTING ON FABRIC

In Europe, block printing on fabric was practised as early as the thirteenth century. However, in the eighteenth and nineteenth centuries, huge factories were built to produce cloth in large quantities. It became cheaper and easier to print patterns by machine.

▲ *This fabric print, called* The Strawberry Thief, *was designed by William Morris in 1883.*

In 1881, a British **designer** called William Morris and some of his friends set up a company to revive the craft of hand block printing. The designs for their prints were based on the plants and birds in the countryside around their homes. They also took ideas from **illuminated manuscripts** and other decorative objects from the Middle Ages. The fabric was printed using blocks, but it was so skilfully done that the join lines were almost invisible. The ideas of William Morris spread to Europe and the USA, where other artists and craftspeople started producing prints using the same kind of hand blocks.

In the 1930s, the British painters Phyllis Barron and Dorothy Larcher took up hand block printing after finding some old printing blocks in a French market. Eventually they set up a specialist printing workshop.

▼ *A hand block printed fabric designed by Phyllis Barron and Dorothy Larcher.*

Enid Marx, who learnt hand block printing from Barron and Larcher, was very successful. In the 1930s she designed the fabric for the seats on the London Underground.

In India there is a strong **tradition** of hand block printing which goes back many centuries. The **technique** is still widely practised today, and clothes made of Indian hand printed fabric are sold around the world. Although hand printing takes many hours of work, **wages** in India are low, so cloth can still be produced cheaply.

▲ *Enid Marx made block prints using bold simple shapes and colours.*

▼ *This delicate hand printed Indian cloth was made in the nineteenth century.*

A detail from a piece of modern block printed cotton from Rajasthan, northern India. ▶

▼ *Block printing is a slow, time-consuming job.*

BLOCK PRINTING ON PAPER

Many artists use the technique of block printing. They make a limited number of prints from the same block. Each print is numbered and the total number of prints in the **edition** is shown.

In Europe, block printing has been used to make pictures and book illustrations since the fifteenth century. The German Albrecht Dürer was a skilful artist and print-maker, working in the late-fourteenth and early-fifteenth centuries. His **woodcuts** have been studied by other artists and have helped them understand the many ways of block printing.

▲ *A woodcut by Albrecht Dürer. The rhinoceros has been skilfully cut to suggest a suit of armour.*

◄ *A woodcut by twentieth-century German artist Ernst Kirchner. Kirchner gouged out big chunks of wood to make a bold, powerful statement.*

Over the centuries, different materials and techniques have been developed. Very hard wood, such as boxwood, cut using fine, pointed tools, produces crisp, delicate lines. Soft wood can be cut freely in any direction to give bold, lively designs. Pieces of **linoleum** are used to make linocuts. The design is gouged out of the linoleum to produce bold shapes.

▲ *Hard woods are chosen to make wood engravings. These woods allow the artist to use very sharp tools to cut crisp lines, close together.*

▲ *Linocuts produce strong, bold shapes. This one, by Edward Bawden, tells the story of* The Ant and the Grasshopper *from* Aesop's Fables.

In the nineteenth century hand **presses** were used to make posters involving both words and pictures. The letters were created from individual pieces of wooden **type**. The illustrations were **engraved** in wooden blocks.

Often, prints are deliberately made using one colour only – usually black ink on white paper. A special feature of block printing is that the spaces between the shapes are as important as the shapes themselves. The strong contrast between the black and white shows this design feature at its best.

▲ *In the eighteenth and nineteenth centuries, the Japanese made beautiful multicoloured prints.*

The Japanese have a long tradition of coloured block printing. Prints were made using a number of blocks, inked up with different colours. Each block was printed one on top of the other to create a multi-coloured picture. A whole team of experts was involved in the process.

FINDING PRINTING BLOCKS

There are many things that you can use as printing blocks. Look around your house, garden, classroom and school grounds. Look for things with an interesting surface or **texture**.

TURN TO PAGES 16-17 TO FIND OUT ABOUT INKING UP YOUR PRINTING BLOCK.

1 Find objects that can be used as printing blocks just as they are: your hand, a piece of screwed-up paper, a block of rough wood, a bulldog clip, a cork, a piece of sponge.

2 Experiment with vegetables and fruit. For example, cut an apple, pear or onion in half, lengthways or widthways. Wipe the surface dry and ink it up.

3 The firm flesh of a potato can be carved to make a printing block. Cut a potato in half and use a craft knife to cut away parts of the flesh.

Keep the shapes big and bold. Dry the surface carefully before inking and printing. If it is too wet the ink will not take.

Remember: always be careful when using a craft knife.

PAGES 28-9 SHOW YOU HOW TO USE YOUR BLOCK TO BUILD UP REPEATING PATTERNS.

MAKING PRINTING BLOCKS

Many objects have interesting shapes and textures, but they are too flat or flimsy to use just as you find them. For example, find feathers, leaves, keys, pieces of lace, wire mesh or sacking. There are lots of possibilities, but avoid objects with sharp or spiky surfaces.

MAKING A BLOCK USING FOUND OBJECTS

1 Find a block of wood or a small box, such as a matchbox.

2 Cover the surface with glue. Use good strong glue, such as PVA, which is not soluble in water once it is dry.

3 Place the object you want to print on the glue and leave it to dry.

TURN TO PAGES 16-17 TO FIND OUT ABOUT INKING UP YOUR PRINTING BLOCKS.

DESIGNING AND MAKING YOUR OWN BLOCKS

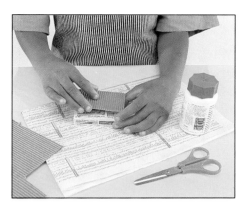

1 Find things that will give a raised surface when stuck on a block – for example, toothpicks, pieces of spaghetti or a length of string.

2 Experiment with different ways of arranging them.

3 When you are pleased with the picture or pattern you have designed, cover the surface of a block of wood with PVA glue and stick the pieces in place. Make several blocks and build up patterns.

PAGES 28-9 SHOW YOU HOW TO USE YOUR BLOCKS TO BUILD UP REPEATING PATTERNS.

MAKING A PAPER BLOCK

1 Take a piece of thin card for the base of the block.

3 Glue the layers down firmly on the base card, one on top of the other.

5 Take a print by laying a sheet of paper on the block and rolling over the back of the paper firmly with a clean roller.

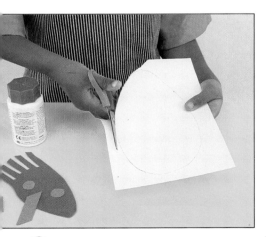

2 Cut strong, simple shapes and bold lines from sugar paper.

4 Ink up the block using oil-based inks. Do not use water-based inks.

MAKING CUT-OUT BLOCKS

POLYSTYRENE BLOCKS

1 Find some blocks of polystyrene. You need the sort used to pack new electrical equipment such as radios and fridges.

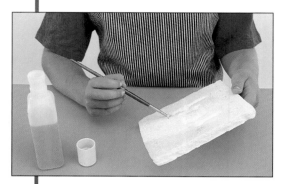

2 Paint a design on a piece of the polystyrene with nail varnish remover. **Be careful not to spill any.** The nail varnish remover will dissolve any areas of the polystyrene that it touches.

3 Ink the block up. The pattern you made will show up as white space. The remaining surface will print in colour.

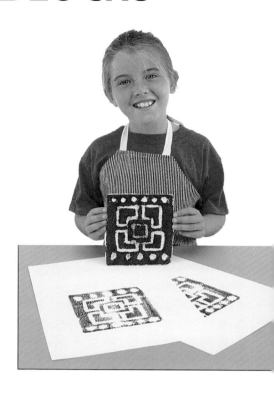

CARVED POTATOES

shown on page 11, where parts of the potato are cut away to make a raised block.

Remember: always be careful when using a craft knife.

Cut a potato in half and use a craft knife to carve shapes into the surface. The design you cut will print white. This is different from the potato block

PLASTICINE BLOCKS

1 Use a glass bottle or an old rolling pin to roll out a block of Plasticine about 3 cm deep. Make the block as flat and level as you can.

Note: Plasticine is greasy. It can reject water-based ink. Mixing the ink with washing-up liquid helps.

2 Cut the block to any size and shape that you want, using a table knife.

3 Press objects with interesting shapes firmly into the block. For example, use screws, wire, wire mesh, keys, paperclips or buttons. When you remove each object its shape will be pressed into the block.

4 Ink the block and make a print. The shapes will be white on a coloured background.

PRINTING INKS AND PAINTS

Printing ink is available in tubes or tubs from art suppliers. It is especially good if you are using a roller to apply colour to your block, because it spreads out thinly and evenly.

There are two kinds of printing ink – water-based and oil-based. Water-based inks are easily cleaned from the block, whereas oil-based inks have to be cleaned off with white spirit. However, if your block is at all greasy it will repel water-based ink. You can avoid this problem by mixing a little washing-up liquid into the ink.

Paint is a good substitute for printing ink, particularly when you are using your block as a stamp. Make up some powder paint into a thick mixture and add a little wallpaper paste. Alternatively, use ready-mixed poster paint and wallpaper paste. Do not use paint with card or paper blocks. It will make them go soggy and disintegrate.

'Inking up' is the special term used for covering the printing block – whether with ink or paint. You can ink up a block using a brush, roller or pad.

MAKING AN INK PAD

1 Find a deep tin lid or margarine tub. Cut a layer of foam sponge to fit.

2 Put the ink or paint into the container. Leave it for a few minutes. The sponge will soak up the ink.

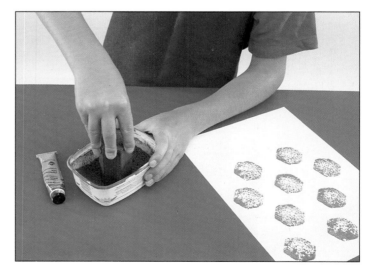

3 Stamp your block down on the pad. It will take up an even covering of ink, ready for printing.

4 Prepare a different coloured printing pad for each colour you are going to use.

USING A ROLLER

4 Roll the ink smoothly on to the block.

5 Place a sheet of paper on the block and roll over it with a clean roller.

6 Prepare a different inking slab for each colour you use.

1 Use a smooth, flat sheet of glass or metal (an old baking tray will do) as an inking slab. Put it on a pad of old newspapers.

2 Put a small dot of ink on the slab. Remember that you always need much less ink than you think. Roll it out thinly and evenly to cover the slab.

3 Now you are ready to ink up your block. The roller will have a thin, even coat of ink on it.

COLOUR PRINTING

You may wish to print a design using more than one colour. The easiest way to do this is to use two or more printing blocks, inked with different colours, to build up a repeating pattern.

Another method is to overprint the image several times in different colours. For this you need several different blocks, all the same size. You can also overprint using the same block, but gradually cut away different parts of the design. A different colour is used after each cut. Obviously, the problem with this method is that it destroys the block.

If you are going to overprint using several blocks, you must make sure they all print exactly on top of each other. If the blocks are not properly **registered**, the image will be blurred.

▲ *This print was made using half a swede. The swede was cut into, inked up with different colours and overprinted several times.*

OVERPRINTING

1 Make an accurate, coloured drawing of how you want your finished print to look.

2 Make several tracings from the drawing, one for each of the colours. Check you have done this correctly by placing the sheets of tracing paper on top of each other. They should match up together exactly.

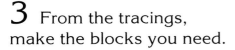

3 From the tracings, make the blocks you need.

4 Cut a cardboard base, 2 cm bigger all round than your printing blocks.

5 Take a second piece of card, cut to the same size. Place a block in the centre and draw round it. Cut out the centre to make a hole exactly the same size as your printing blocks. Stick this card on the base.

6 Ink up the first block and place it in the card mount.

7 Using a piece of printing paper cut to exactly the same size as the base, take a print of the first block.

8 Ink up the second block and place it on the base. Again, position your printing paper exactly on the base and take a print.

9 Do the same with the third block.

PRINTING ON FABRIC

1 Choose a plain fabric with a close **weave**. Cotton fabric, such as unbleached calico, gives good results.

2 Wash the fabric carefully and let it dry. This is important if the fabric is new, because the **finish** put on at the factory may stop the ink taking evenly.

3 Prepare a printing table. Cover a table top with old blankets. Wrap them over the edges and fasten underneath. Cover this with a sheet of polythene and layers of newspaper.

4 Using masking tape, secure the fabric you are going to print to the newspaper. Make sure it is completely flat and unwrinkled.

5 Use special fabric printing ink (available from art suppliers), or the same printing ink or paint-and-paste mixture used for paper (see page 16). If you are making something that you will want to wash, you will need to choose a waterproof colour, such as an oil-based ink.

8 Start by making something fairly small, such as a scarf or handkerchief. Once you have got the idea, go on to print enough fabric to make an apron or cushion covers.

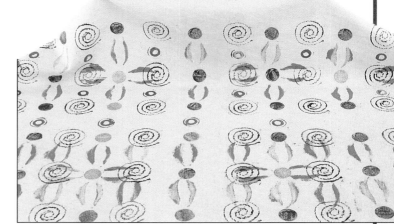

To print a ▶ *large piece of fabric, such as a tablecloth, fold the cloth and iron in the folds. This will help you print in straight lines.*

6 Use any of the different sorts of printing blocks described on pages 10-15. Plasticine blocks are particularly suitable for use on fabric. Fruit and vegetable blocks give good results. Prints are always stamped on to fabric: the blocks are placed ink-side down on the cloth.

▼ *Some of the things you can make using block printed fabric (clockwise from top): a cushion cover; a long silk scarf; a cotton handkerchief; a square silk scarf.*

TURN TO PAGES 24-5 FOR IDEAS ABOUT USING PRINTED FABRIC.

7 To print a large piece of fabric, it is helpful to choose a block that can be mounted on wood so that it lasts longer. It may help to use a wooden mallet to tap the block down lightly on to the fabric.

PROJECTS USING PAPER

Collect a range of different papers. Some will be more suited to printing wrapping paper, others to cards or posters.

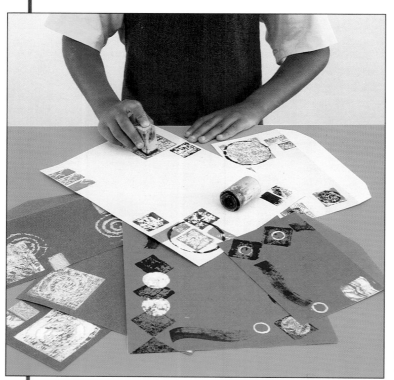

2 Make greetings cards by printing on to stiff paper or card, folded in half. If you want to make a large number of cards, for instance at Christmas, set up a **production team** (see posters project).

1 Print your own writing paper and envelopes. Print borders on the writing paper, leaving enough space for writing. Envelopes can have a more overall design, but leave space for the address. Also, try using a word processor to design and print a heading for the writing paper. Then print up the borders.

3 Make wrapping paper and matching gift tags. Use a printing block to build up a repeating pattern for the wrapping paper. Turn to pages 28-9 for ideas about building up patterns. Make matching gift tags by printing the same design on to card. Alternatively, cut a piece off the bottom of the printed sheet and stick it on to card.

POSTERS

1 With a group of friends, make a poster to advertise a special event, such as a play, concert, or car-boot sale. Organize yourselves into a production team to design and print an edition of about ten posters.

2 Decide what the poster needs to say. Use as few words as possible, but be sure to include all the important details: the name of the event, the date, the time, the address, where to get tickets, the cost.

3 Discuss how you can use block printing to make the posters look attractive. Make several designs and discuss which one will work best. Leave a space in the centre to stick the text.

4 Use a word processor to write the text. Print it out and enlarge the type on a photocopier to the size you need. Make ten copies.

5 Print the design on to the poster. Organize yourselves into an **assembly line**, with different people responsible for printing the different colours in the design. Stick the text in the centre of each poster.

Wed 3rd September

HARVEST SUPPER

6pm in the
SCHOOL HALL
Tickets £3 from
Mrs Patel Tel 2304

A Project Using Fabric

Gather together a group of friends to make some curtains. These could be for a room in your school or for some other local public building. Do not choose a very large window. In your group, include someone who is good at maths, someone with good design skills, and someone who can sew.

Making a Pair of Block Printed Curtains

1 Visit the room with your team. Discuss who uses the room, when and why. Try to talk to these people about what they like. Look at the colours in the room already. With this in mind, discuss the design and colours for the curtains.

2 Draw up several ideas. Make blocks for the idea you like best. Test it out by printing it on paper.

3 Decide how much fabric you will need. Take careful measurements of the window. Measure the length from top to bottom of the frame, then add 40 cm. This will allow for turnings at the top and bottom, plus extra to make sure the finished curtains cover the frame well.

Measurements for each curtain:

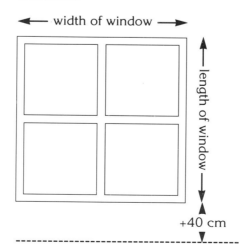

← width of window →

length of window

+40 cm

4 Measure the width of the window. Curtains look best if they are gathered in folds, so for a pair of curtains, make sure each one is at least the width of the window. Fabric is sold in standard widths. Most windows will need two widths of fabric sewn together to make each curtain.

5 Multiply the number of widths you need by the length of the window. This gives the length of fabric needed.

6 Now work out the cost of the project. Multiply the cost of the fabric per metre by the number of metres you need. **Estimate** how many tubes of printing ink you will need.

7 Now that you have a design and a cost, discuss the project with a responsible adult to get approval. Agree a plan for paying for the project.

8 Prepare a large printing table and print all the fabric you need.

11 Attach curtain hooks and put the curtains up. Allow them to hang for a week. Then pin up the bottom and hem it.

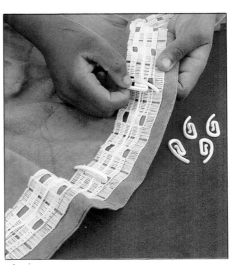

10 Turn under the top edge, and pin on some curtain heading tape. Sew in place with a sewing machine.

9 Now make up the curtains. If you are using two widths for each curtain, sew them together, matching the patterns carefully. Hem the sides.

THE GALLERY

Look around you for ideas for print designs. Look out for bold shapes and things that will give crisp, clean results. Make sketches and take photographs of the things you see.

On pages 10-15 there are suggestions for objects to collect and make into printing blocks. The pictures here give some ideas for patterns to design, using your printing blocks.

▲ *A row of railings.*

▼ *Brickwork.*

▲ *Ducks against the setting sun.*

A bunch of grapes. ▶

▲ *Straight lines of cut corn.*

◄ *Holes in a metal bench.*

A spotted fish. ►

▼ *Bold strawberry shapes.*

MAKING PATTERNS

Once you have designed and made a printing block, you can start experimenting with it to build up regular and **random** patterns.

First, experiment by repeating a single block, using one colour only. The amount of white space between the prints is very important. The same block can give very different results, depending on how close together or far apart you place the repeats. Also, each print you make will be slightly different. Sometimes it will be full of ink, sometimes it will be dry. This all adds to the effect. Here are some different ways of building up patterns.

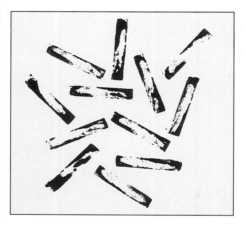

◀ *Random repeats.*

Half-drop repeats. ▶

▼ *Regular repeats.*

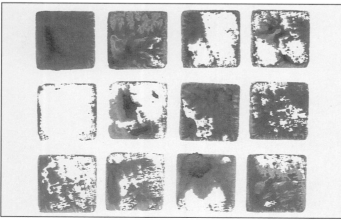

▼ *Square brick repeats.*

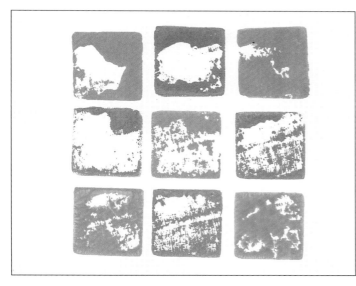

▲ *Now try introducing a second colour.*

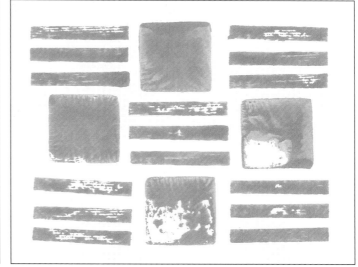

▲ *Introduce a second printing block.*

This panel was made using six different blocks and overprinting them in different colours. With block printing, you can overprint light colours on dark ink. ▶

GLOSSARY

Assembly line A group of people working together to get a job done quickly, for example in a factory. Each person is responsible for a stage of the process.

Civilizations Groups of people who form a state with a highly organized structure and culture. Civilizations that existed thousands of years ago are called ancient civilizations.

Designer A person who works out the shape and style of an object or decoration.

Edition In printing, an edition is the entire number of copies made.

Engraved Carved into a block of wood or metal plate so that a print can be made.

Estimate Calculate roughly.

Fabric Cloth.

Finish A special surface put on a piece of cloth, to change the way it looks or feels.

Illuminated manuscripts Books written out by hand and highly decorated. They were made in the Middle Ages, before people knew how to print books.

Image Picture.

Linoleum A floor covering made of canvas coated with solid linseed oil.

Presses Machines used for printing.

Production team A group of people, each with special skills, who work together to design and make something.

Random Without any plan or order.

Registered Correctly lined up.

Run A number of prints from the same block or blocks.

Seals Small, carved objects which can be pressed into a soft substance to make a mark.

Tablets Slabs of stone, clay or wood. In the past they were used for writing on.

Technique Method or skill.

Texture The feel of an object's surface.

Tradition A custom that has been practised over many years, by one generation of people after another.

Type A small block of metal or wood with a letter on it, used for printing words.

Wages The money a worker earns.

Weave The pattern made by weaving. This is a method of making fabric by pushing cross threads under and over vertical threads.

Woodcuts Prints made using a block of wood which has a design carved into it.

FURTHER INFORMATION

BOOKS TO READ

Devonshire, Hilary *Printing* (Franklin Watts, 1988)

O'Reilly, Susie *Textiles* (Wayland, 1991)

Singer, Margo and Spyrou, Mary *Textile Art, Multicultural Traditions* (A & C Black, 1989)

Tofts, Hannah *The Print Book* (Franklin Watts/Two-Can, 1990)

PLACES TO VISIT

Britain
The Museum of Mankind
6 Burlington Gardens
London
W1X 2EX

The Victoria and Albert
   Museum
Cromwell Road
South Kensington
London
SW7 2RL

Australia
Victoria State Craft
   Collection
Meat Market Craft Centre
Courtney Street North
Victoria 3051

Canada
Montreal Museum of Fine
   Arts
1379 Sherbrooke Street
   West
Montreal
Quebec
H3B 3E1

Royal Ontario Museum
100 Queen's Park
Toronto
Ontario
M5S 2C6

For further information about arts and crafts, contact the following organizations:

The Crafts Council
44A Pentonville Road
London
N1 9BY
UK

Crafts Council of New
   Zealand
22 The Terrace
Wellington
PO Box 498
Wellington Island
New Zealand

INDEX

ACKNOWLEDGEMENTS

The publishers would like to thank the following for allowing their photographs to be reproduced: Bridgeman Art Library 5 left, 6 left, 7 bottom left, 8 bottom, 9 top left (Chelmsford Museums Service); E. T. Archive 4 bottom, 8 top, 9 top right, 9 bottom; Eye Ubiquitous title page, 7 centre right, 7 bottom right (L. Goffin), 26 top right (P. Prestidge), 27 bottom left; Holburne Museum and Crafts Study Centre, Bath 6 right, 7 top; Michael Holford 4 top; Tony Stone Worldwide 5 right (Osmond), 26 left (C. Harvey), 26 centre (G. Kohler), 26 right (D. Bassett), 27 top (A. Sacks); Zefa 27 centre right (R. Morsch), 27 bottom right (L. Lefever). All other photographs, including cover, were supplied by Zul Mukhida. Logo artwork was supplied by John Yates.

The linocut *Woman with a Hat*, by Pablo Picasso, appears by permission of the copyright holders © DACS 1993.

The fabric prints *Winchester*, by Phyllis Barron and Dorothy Larcher, and *Hail*, by Enid Marx, appear by permission of the Holburne Museum and Crafts Study Centre, Bath.

The linocut *The Ant and the Grasshopper*, by Edward Bawden, appears by permission of the estate of Edward Bawden.